KEYBOARD

Amazing Phrasing

50 WAYS TO IMPROVE YOUR IMPROVISATIONAL SKILLS

BY DEBBIE DENKE

ISBN 0-634-02619-4

HAL•LEONARD® CORPORATION

7777 W. BLUEMOUND RD. P.O. BOX 13819 MILWAUKEE, WI 53213

Visit Hal Leonard Online at
www.halleonard.com

Also available by Debbie Denke:
The Aspiring Jazz Pianist
(HL00290480)

Contents

Introduction

Chords, scales, patterns... When many of us think of improvisation, these are what come to mind. But these tools—although they're important—are only part of the process of improvising. *Amazing Phrasing* is your guide to the rest. Think of this as a sourcebook of ideas and a guide to keep you moving forward on the right path.

Amazing Phrasing is for all keyboard players interested in learning how to improvise and how to improve their creative phrasing. This method is divided into three parts:

- **Melody**

  Covering scales, arpeggios, licks, riffs, runs, and playing "outside," this first section focuses on melodic strategies for improvisation. Wondering what to do with your right hand when it's time for you to take the lead? Not sure how to build a solo from start to finish? Here's where to begin.

- **Harmony**

  Whether comping or soloing, harmony is essential to improvisation, and this section covers it. Need to harmonize a melody in your right hand? Want to learn to comp with your left hand while soloing with your right? Need some common chord progressions to practice? How about some two-handed voicings for your combo playing? Want to add chord extensions or create a bass line?

- **Rhythm & Style**

  Whether you want to swing, lay back, or shape your phrases with accents, this last section puts the finishing touches on your improvisational technique. You'll learn approaches to working with and around other musicians, and you'll practice comping and soloing over progressions in various styles—from rock to bossa nova to swing to bebop.

Although this book is intended to be read from start to finish, feel free to skip around as you like. *Amazing Phrasing* is chock full of ideas, and the companion CD will help you learn the concepts and apply them. The CD contains demos for listening, as well as many play-along examples so you can practice improvising over various musical styles and progressions. Listen to the examples first, and then remove the recorded piano tracks by turning the balance knob to the left in order to supply your own phrases.

Amazing Phrasing is designed to send you on your way toward discovering your own creative voice and unique way of improvising. Enjoy the journey!

Melodic Embellishment

Idea

Improvisation is spontaneous composition. Although jazz musicians are probably the masters of improvisation today, they were not the inventors of it. Most cultures have in their musical history some form of improvised music, and improvisation has been a keyboard tradition for centuries. In fact, Bach and Beethoven were masters of the art, as were many other keyboardists from the Baroque and Classical eras.

The early improvisers played around primarily with the melody of a tune. This is what's known as *melodic embellishment*. The use of spontaneous ornamental devices in traditional European art music dates back as far as Gregorian chant in the 7th century. If you were a keyboard player during Bach's time, it was generally assumed that you would interpret the melody in your own way by embellishing it with ornaments such as trills, turns, neighboring tones, and other decorations. These devices were used not only to allow for some creativity on the part of the performer, but also to help prolong the short tone of the harpsichord! It wasn't until later that these devices became standardized and formally written out, with improvisation (except in the occasional cadenza) eventually becoming suppressed among the "serious" composers and performers.

In the music of today, we still use some of these ornamental devices. Notice how the Lennon/McCartney tune "A Day in the Life" and Grover Washington Jr.'s "Mr. Magic" make use of the *trill*. Hear how Clifford Brown's "Joy Spring" and Horace Silver's "Song for My Father" contain *turns*. The Harry Warren composition "Serenade in Blue" uses lots of *neighboring tones*, while Thelonious Monk's "Blue Monk" and Debussy's "Afternoon of a Faun" contain *passing tones*. Dizzy Gillespie reused the harmony to an old standard named "Whispering" and replaced it with his own melody—a device called *contrafaction*. Dizzy's new tune, "Groovin' High," is loaded with *target notes*. Other devices that date back hundreds of years and are still being used by today's improvisers include *inverting the melody* and *altering the rhythm*.

Let's take a look at how we can apply the aforementioned melodic embellishments to a familiar tune. If you open up a hymnal to "Amazing Grace," you'll find a basic melody similar to this (with slightly different lyrics!):

TRACK 1

Here's what the same tune might look like if the melody were embellished. (The harmony has also been changed here to include more complex chords, making the tune even more fun and interesting.) This is only one of the many ways to rephrase "Amazing Grace."

TRACK 2

Here's an explanation of the melodic embellishments used:

Trill	Rapid alternation between a given note and the note a step above
Turn	Notes that revolve around a given note
Neighboring tones	Notes that move stepwise to either side of a given note
Passing tones	Notes that pass between two given notes
Target notes	Notes that approach a given note first from above, then below
Inversion	The opposite direction of the original melody (upside down)
Altering rhythm	Variation in the duration, entrances, and repetition of notes

Track 3 runs through this version of "Amazing Grace" again, this time with bass and drums added. It also includes three more improvised variations, wrapping up with a restatement of the main melody.

Listen to this track, and then try your own version. Line up track 3 again and move the balance knob on your sound system to the left in order to remove the piano and supply your own phrases. It's OK to play with just your right hand embellishing the melody, but if you know how to play the chords, go ahead and include them in your left hand. (For more on chord voicings, see the *Harmony* section of this book.) Play five variations of this tune. At the very end, repeat the last four bars as a tag, as shown.

TRACK 3

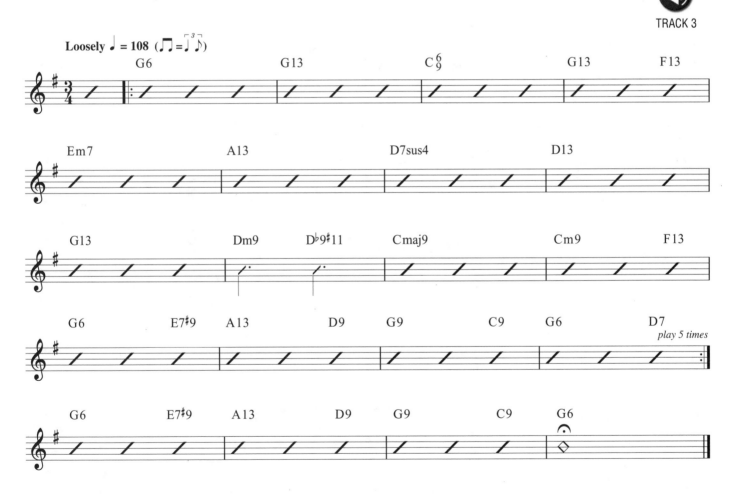

Go ahead and move the balance knob back to the center for future demos in this book. Whenever you wish to play along, crank it over to the left and jam with the band.

Arpeggios

*Idea #*2

Another handy thing for you to know as an improviser is that, in addition to embellishing the melody, you can *always* play with the chord tones. Somebody in the band is playing the chords—chances are it's you! And since the chords are already being played in your left hand, it makes sense that if you improvise in your right hand with the corresponding chord tones, they won't clash. In fact, they'll sound great!

Here's a set of three exercises to get you started arpeggiating chords. Apply these to any tune you wish to improvise over, in any style—from the most basic country to the wildest bebop. The examples shown all use the same four-bar chord progression with various voicings and time signatures; naturally, you would change the chords to suit whatever piece you're currently working on.

Exercise #1: *Arpeggiate up.* Start with the root, and arpeggiate the first four chord tones: root, third, fifth, and seventh. Use eighth notes for rhythm. Notice what to do when there are two chords per measure:

TRACK 4

Exercise #2: *Arpeggiate down.* Reverse the order, starting this time with the top note:

TRACK 5

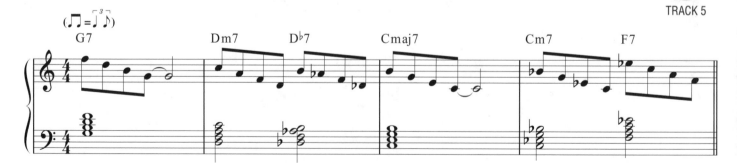

Exercise #3: *Mix and match.* This is when it gets fun! With this step, you're really improvising because you're making *choices*. For instance, you might choose to go up one chord and down another. If you want to take this to the next level, try using inversions in the RH. Play with all four chord tones, or just one. Vary the rhythms, use rests, repeat some notes, and explore the different ranges of the keyboard.

Notice the LH rhythmic variety in the following example, which is only one of the many ways to illustrate this exercise:

TRACK 6

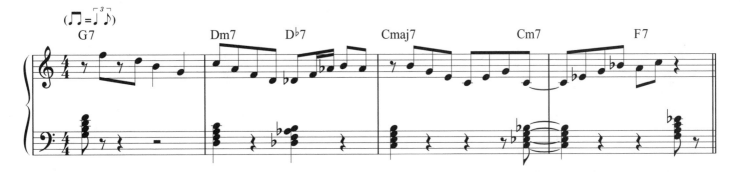

3/4 Time

What if your piece isn't in 4/4 time? This exercise uses a 3/4 beat. The second chords in bars 2 and 4 are arpeggiated with sixteenth notes to fit the 3/4 rhythm:

TRACK 7

Now start with the top note and arpeggiate downward in 3/4 time.

The following is one possible outcome for exercise #3 in 3/4 time:

TRACK 8

Complex Voicings

Here's an advanced way to apply arpeggios for those who know how to play rootless left-hand voicings with upper chord extensions. During exercise #1, arpeggiate with your right hand the same chord voicings that your left hand is playing, but one octave higher:

TRACK 9

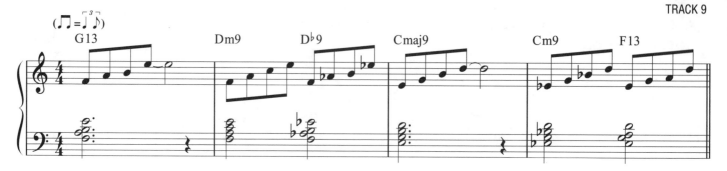

Here's one way to apply exercise #3 with complex voicings:

TRACK 10

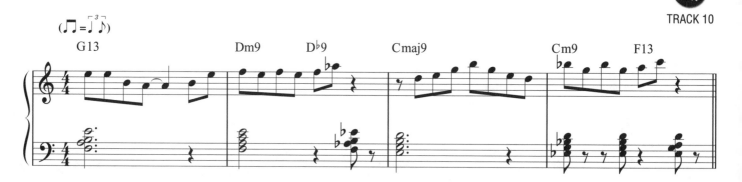

If you ever run into a piece with more than two chords per measure, choose to arpeggiate the two chords that fall closest to beats 1 and 3.

Be sure to practice these exercises over the whole form of the piece, and don't skip any steps or repeated chords in your piece. If you try to cut corners and save time, you won't be doing yourself any favors in the long run. Remember, developing a good sense of form is extremely important!

The Scale/Chord Approach

Idea #3

Perhaps you've heard about an improvisational approach that assigns a specific scale for every chord played. You know that early improvisers played around with the melodies of tunes, and later came the idea that the basic chord tones could always be used as pleasant-sounding note choices. But how did they come up with all these ideas about corresponding scales that go with each and every chord?

To answer that question, we must go back and look at some music history. During the late 19th and early 20th century, Western music's harmony became much more complex. Composers like Claude Debussy and other impressionists began using chords that contained ninths, elevenths, and thirteenths (known as upper-chord *extensions*). These tones were also sometimes *altered* (raised or lowered by a half step).

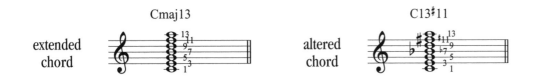

If you take a complex chord like the C13#11 in the above example and rearrange the tones, you'll find that these tones can be put in consecutive order to form a scale:

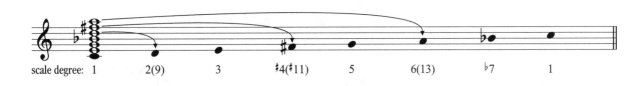

Music theorists have the benefit of hindsight to observe which tones musicians have successfully used during improvisation. Bebop musicians such as alto saxophonist Charlie Parker played with upper chord extensions similar to those in the above scale/chord example. This became part of the bebop sound. The music theorists then gave this particular scale its own name: *C Lydian dominant.* This is why today it is now recommended to use the C Lydian dominant scale when improvising over a C13#11 in a bebop style.

There are hundreds of different scales, each with their own particular sound and use over various chords. Often, more than one scale may be used with a given chord depending on the improviser's taste, the style and mood of the tune, and the surrounding harmony. The next several "ideas" will give the most useful scales to get you started.

The Major Scale

*Idea #*4

The first and most important scale to learn for improvisation is the major scale. All other scales are typically compared to it.* It's also probably the most familiar sounding scale to our ears (do–re–mi–fa–so–la–ti–do). Here's the C major scale:

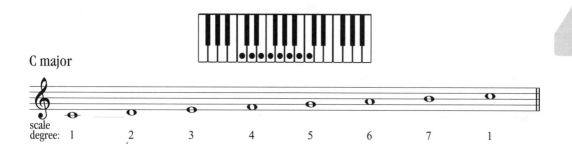

C major

scale degree: 1 2 3 4 5 6 7 1

Notice that the major scale follows a specific sequence of steps between each note:

C   D   E   F   G   A   B   C
whole whole half whole whole whole half

Rather than counting by whole and half steps, it would probably be easiest and best to just learn what the flats and sharps are in each major scale. If you don't already know all of your major scales, learn them *at least* in the right hand (the main hand used for improvising) two octaves up and down, in all twelve keys. Practice them in this order (moving down by fifths):

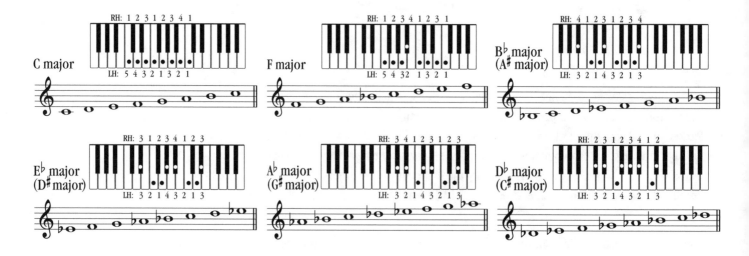

* Music theorists will often describe another scale by saying something like, "This particular scale resembles the major scale, with the exception of a lowered third and lowered seventh, blah blah blah."

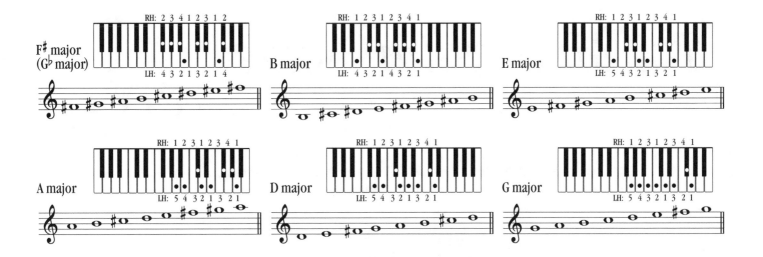

Also try them in the following sequences:

C, C#, D, D#, E, F, F#, G, G#, A, A#, B, C (moving up by half steps)

C, B, B♭, A, A♭, G, G♭, F, E, E♭, D, D♭, C (moving down by half steps)

Learn your major scales with the proper fingering; put in your time. It will be well worth it. (You won't need to be as concerned with properly fingering all of the other types of scales.)

Use phrases based on the corresponding major scale (e.g., the C major scale for C chords, the F major scale for F chords, and so on) when you encounter the following chord types:

most **major triads** (example: **C**)

major sixth chords (C6)

major seventh chords (Cmaj7)

One final word of advice: Beware of the fourth tone in each major scale. It requires special handling to sound good. Either avoid using that note, play it quickly in a sequential pattern, or resolve it immediately to the third tone of the scale. If you're sure you are playing with the right scale tones but hear a "green"-sounding note, you can bet it is the fourth. Resolve it quickly, and the sting of that sound will disappear.

The Mixolydian Scale

Idea #5

The next scale you need to know is the *Mixolydian scale*. (Yes, it is a bulky-sounding name, and you can call it "the dominant scale" if you prefer.) This scale resembles the major scale with a lowered seventh:

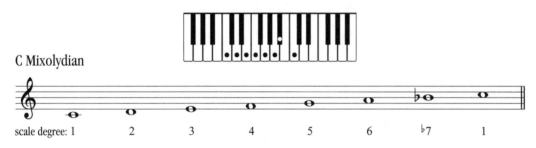

C Mixolydian

scale degree: 1   2   3   4   5   6   ♭7   1

The Mixolydian scale can also be seen as using the *same* notes as the major scale located a fifth below. For example, C Mixolydian contains the same notes as the F major scale, but starts instead on the root note of C.

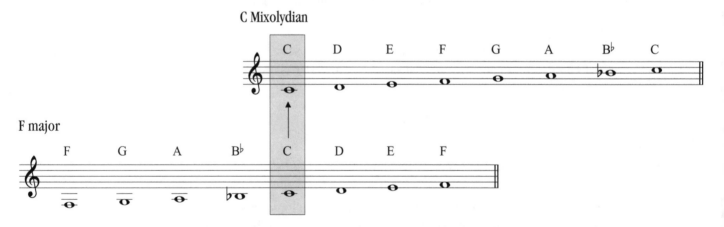

C Mixolydian

F major

Therefore, if you know your major scales, you can easily figure out the notes for the Mixolydian scales. Practice the Mixolydian scales (after you have become thoroughly aquainted with the major scales) in the same order as before, moving by fifths and chromatically.

Make phrases based on selected notes from the corresponding Mixolydian scales when you encounter the following chords:

certain **major triads (C)** in rock or blues style

dominant seventh chords (C7)

sus chords (C7sus4)

ninth chords (C9)

thirteenth chords (C13)

Once again, watch out how you handle the fourth tone in these scales, too!

The Dorian Scale

Idea #

6

There are many types of minor scales. Concert pianists practice the natural, harmonic, and melodic minor scales because they occur most often in classical music. However, the most frequently used minor scale in jazz, pop, and contemporary music of today is the *Dorian* minor scale. Compared to the major scale, Dorian has both a lowered third and lowered seventh:

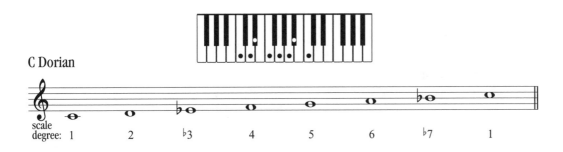

It's probably easiest to think of the Dorian scale as having the same notes as the major scale located one whole step below. In other words, C Dorian has the same notes as B♭ major, only starting on the note C. They both contain the notes B♭ and E♭.

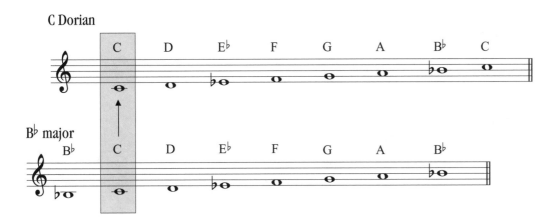

Create phrases based on the Dorian scale for the following chords:

most **minor triads (Cm)**

minor sixth chords (Cm6)

minor seventh chords (Cm7)

minor ninth chords (Cm9)

minor eleventh chords (Cm11)

The Dorian scale works well over nearly 80 percent of the minor chords used today. Don't worry about resolving the fourth tone; it will sound fine in this scale.

The Blues Scale

Idea # 7

The blues scale is extremely useful for many forms of music, including jazz, rock, and, of course, rhythm 'n' blues! The blues scale may be used whenever you want to get that soulful/funky/bluesy sound. Often when musicians get together for the first time, they'll jam on the blues to get musically acquainted. Learn to play the blues in several keys. The keys of G, C, F, B♭, and E♭ are recommended for jazz musicians (horn players like these keys). If you plan on playing with rock guitarists, learn the blues in E, A, D, G, and C.

Here's the traditional six-note blues scale. As you can see, there are large gaps between some of the notes, while other notes are very close together. Some of the tones are deliberately dissonant, which give this scale a desired "in the cracks" sound.

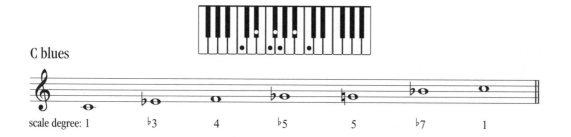

C blues

scale degree: 1   ♭3   4   ♭5   5   ♭7   1

Make up phrases based on the blues scale in the following situations:

> when playing the **regular or minor blues (C blues or Cm blues)**
>
> *certain* **dominant seventh chords (C7)** for a bluesy sound
>
> *some* **minor seventh chords (Cm7)** for rock/funk tunes

One of the simple beauties about playing the blues is that you don't always have to change to a different scale when the chords change. For instance, when playing a blues in the key of C, you can stick with notes from the C blues scale for the *whole* piece and still sound cool!

The following tune, "The Downer Blues," is a basic 12-bar C blues based on the descending blues scale. Two different sets of chord changes are shown. The first set shows the regular blues progression; the second set is for the minor blues. Notice that the same *head* (melody) works for both sets of chords. Learn to play the head, and then experiment with improvising your own phrases based on the C blues scale:

TRACK 11

The Downer Blues

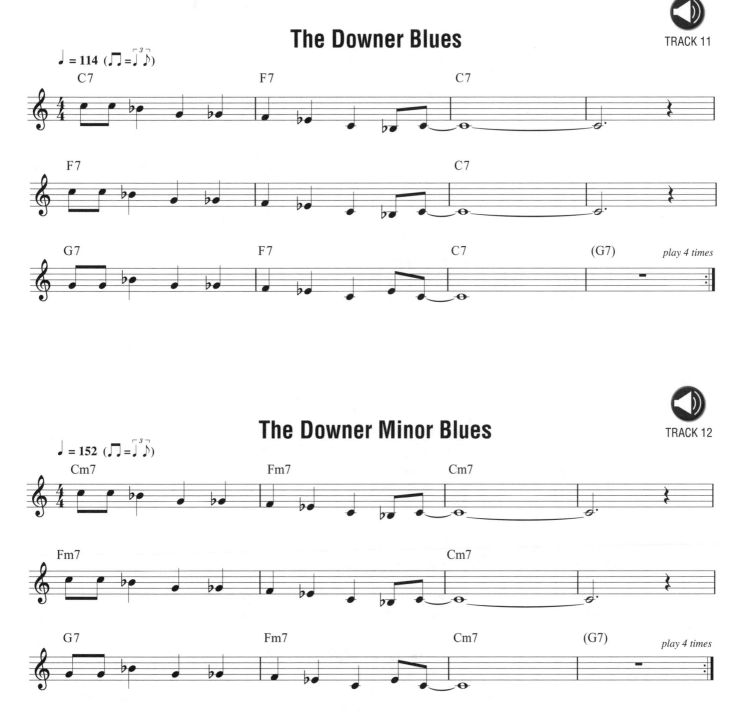

TRACK 12

The Downer Minor Blues

When you see parentheses ( ) around a chord or chords during the last bar of a piece, this means to play these chords only when you plan to repeat the tune. This is called a *turnaround*. The final chorus will end on the previous chord, the tonic of the key.

The "Other" Blues Scale

Idea # 8

Here's an interesting fact that isn't so widely known: There are actually *two* blues scales that will work for improvisation during a regular blues. The first one, built on the root of the key center of your blues, is what you used for "The Downer Blues." A lesser-known (but equally effective) blues scale begins on the root located three half steps lower.

Here's how it works: If you want to play the C blues, you may use either the C blues scale or the A blues scale. Construct this "other" blues scale the same way, using the root (A), lowered third (C), fourth (D), lowered fifth (E♭), fifth (E), and lowered seventh (G) degrees. These two scales contain a few common tones, but the A blues scale adds some extra notes that open up your options for improvisation.

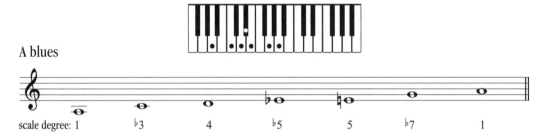

A blues

scale degree: 1   ♭3   4   ♭5   5   ♭7   1

Play the above scale, then try it over the chords of a C blues. You'll hear some brighter-sounding notes. You may wish to experiment with this scale when playing tunes like "C Jam Blues" (Duke Ellington), "In the Mood" (Glenn Miller), and "The Swingin' Shepherd Blues" (Moe Koffman). This particular scale also works well played up high on the keyboard when you desire a Count Basie-style sound. In fact, the two blues scales may be combined to give you a whole lot of choices for phrasing the blues!

My recommendation is this: Use the *original* blues scale for rock, minor blues, and harder-edged tunes; use the *other* blues scale for a sweeter sound.

Now try playing "The Brighter Blues." It's a basic C blues again, but this time the head is made up of tones taken from the A blues scale. Improvise with these notes and enjoy the sounds!

The Brighter Blues

TRACK 13

Repeat last 4 bars for ending

Soloing Melodically

Idea # 9

After you've gotten your tools together by putting in those long hours arpeggiating and learning scales, it's time to make real music out of all this! Technique and knowledge are very important, but there's nothing like a memorable, *melodic* solo. (Of course, in order to add emotion and soul to your solo, you need to make sure lack of technique is not a hindrance. Then it's time to turn your ideas into melodies.)

Be sure you're listening to lots of great improvisers. Even if you cannot feel their influence today, at some time in the future you will be inspired by what you're actively hearing now. Listen not only to keyboard players, but also to horn players and singers for their phrasing. (Hear how Frank Sinatra could rephrase a standard tune—the way he breathed, syncopated, and sustained certain notes.)

Keyboard players should learn how to play lots of melodies to different tunes, even when they're in a group with a lead singer or instrumentalist. Remember that embellishing the original melody during your solo, or even using bits of it, will always work well for improvisation. Besides, you can quote part of the melody of a completely different tune during your solo as long as it fits over the chord changes. (Singer/pianist Diana Krall often interjects quotes during her piano improvisations and gets a knowing chuckle of recognition from the audience for doing so.) Reading and playing melodies is a good thing; transcribing them yourself is even better, because you'll memorize them faster and understand how they were constructed. One more idea: if the tune you're learning has lyrics, learn them. Becoming familiar with the mood of the song will make your phrasing more singable.

The following is a list of things to think about when you're ready to improve your melodic improvisation. Record yourself first to get an objective idea of how you sound, then tackle these ideas one at a time. Make good use of:

Accents	They make you sound confident.
Rests	Breathe! Otherwise, you'll exhaust people's ears.
Repetition	Of pitches and/or rhythms—just don't overdo it.
Skips and steps	Have a good balance between arpeggios and scales.
Range	Don't play all your ideas in the same octave.
Direction of ideas	Avoid having all phrases travel predictably up or down.
Continuity	Use common tones or rhythmic patterns to keep the RH flowing smoothly even as the LH chords change.

Building a Solo

Idea # 10

Once your phrasing starts coming together, it's time to look at the big picture: how to build a solo. A good solo is like a story. It captures the listener's attention at the start, builds interest, and has a climax and a conclusion. The solo should be comprised of phrases of varying length and have elements of both surprise and satisfaction. The solo might also have a certain character, depending on your own style plus the mood of the tune you wish to convey—perhaps humorous, romantic, joyous, tasteful, bluesy, intense, or quirky.

Keep these ideas in mind:

1. Start simply. Don't use up your best ideas in the first eight bars.

2. Use these elements to help build excitement:

    Speed created by faster moving note values
    Begin with half notes and plenty of rests; change to quarters, eighths, triplets, sixteenths, etc.

    Thicker textures
    Build from single notes, to combination tones and octaves, to chords.

    Increasing range
    Start off in the midrange and move up, or else start high and light and move down.

    Volume
    Gradually get louder. Use dynamics!

    Dissonance
    Begin playing inside the harmony, then elect to play more outside, chromatic ideas.

    Tension through repetition
    Use long tremolos, repeated patterns, or notes.

3. The polite way to conclude your solo is to start winding it down during the last few bars. This cues the band that your turn is almost over and it's time for the next soloist to start building their ideas (or to return to the melody). Of course, you may wish to end your solo with a bang (right before a drum solo, perhaps) or with a competitive "top this" attitude. It's your call!

An Attitude of Confidence

Idea # 11

Having the right attitude while improvising is half the battle. When it's your turn in the spotlight, you want to give an impression of confidence—or at least that you're into the music and enjoying the experience. Don't play with a timid touch or back away from strange-sounding, unintended notes. (We won't call them mistakes here!) Remember: you are never further than a half step away from a good-sounding note at all times. Some musicians go so far as to say that there are no wrong notes when improvising; it's simply a matter of how a person approaches the note and gets off of it. End up on a good-sounding note, and you'll leave the listener with a good impression.

Even if you are insecure about improvising, it's important to act as though you know what you're doing—otherwise, you may lose the audition to the guy who exudes confidence but really doesn't play any better than you do!

Licks, Riffs, and Runs

Idea #

12

Many students of improvisation want to know if they should use licks, riffs, runs, and other patterns during their solos. First, let's define some of these terms:

Lick   A phrase that was once improvised but is now is imitated by other musicians, as in, "I'm going to play an Oscar Peterson lick." Certain licks may work well in some keys on the keyboard but are awkward in other keys due to fingering problems. Another example might be, "I'm going to play this black-key lick."

Riff   A repeated idea often used as an accompaniment pattern. Originally, a riff was a horn section figure. Many blues heads are "riff-like."

Run   A scale-like pattern that typically omits a few scale tones. A run is usually played in the same direction, as in a descending run or an ascending run.

Pianists of all types sooner or later develop certain licks, riffs, runs, sequences, or patterns that they like to play. They incorporate them into their phrasing, and these ideas become a part of their recognized style. We first learn by imitating others, and learning patterns can be an acceptable way to get started—as long as the patterns don't become crutches.

Perhaps someone has shown you a cool pattern that would work well during your piano solo in a certain tune. Go ahead and use it if you wish, but the key is to *be flexible.* Stay away from trying to force a pattern into your solo. What if you wanted to begin your improvisation with a special lick that begins on beat 1, but the sax solo before yours didn't end till beat 3? You would be accused of not listening to the horn player and stepping all over him. What if your run begins on high C, but your right hand is playing near middle C? You could really mess yourself up trying to frantically jump to the upper register on time. Try to be spontaneous (that's what improvising is all about), and if your pattern fits, use it. If not, try something else.

There is something to be said, from a learning standpoint, for writing out your own solos beforehand. I once had a teacher who suggested I compose a solo in a bebop style over some basic jazz chord changes in the key of B♭. In doing this exercise, I could slow down and take time to come up with my own patterns and ideas. Then I had to memorize and play my "solo" in not only the original key, but also the remote key of E. From that point on, phrasing in a bebop style felt much more comfortable to me, and I felt proud that I had come up with my own ideas.

Playing Outside

Idea # 13

When a musician deliberately chooses to improvise with notes that are not included in any of the chords or their corresponding scales, this is called *playing outside.* (This doesn't mean an outdoor gig; it just means playing "outside" of the chord changes.) This style only tends to sound good if you know how to confidently play "inside" the chord changes first. Otherwise, you'll sound like a toddler at the keyboard, or worse yet, a person making lots of mistakes!

Playing outside creates intense-sounding music. It's not for everyone, but it can be fun to experiment with. It often works best from a tension/resolution approach. Try playing chromatic ideas, or improvising a half step above the key center, during the high point of your solo, after you've proven that you know what you're doing. Then, before you can't take the dissonance anymore, resolve your phrase by returning to playing inside the chord tones.

Chick Corea is a pianist who can play both inside and outside very effectively. In fact, some of his "outside" playing may be analyzed as very complex harmony, ahead of its time. If you are especially into outside music, check out pianist Cecil Taylor. Often what he improvises has no established key center or chords and can be considered free-form improvisational music. The classical musicians call this style of music *atonal*; jazz musicians call it *avant-garde* or *free jazz.* To some people with conservative musical taste, all contemporary music sounds like this!

Be Tasteful

Idea # 14

I'm going to state the obvious here: Not only should the title and lyrics of a particular tune play a role in determining the style of your playing, but each musical situation needs to be treated with good taste.

Generally speaking, don't add a bunch of complex tones like altered fifths, ninths, elevenths, and thirteenths to your phrases when the brother of the bride wants to do his Elvis impressions at the wedding reception. (If you don't know what I'm talking about, don't worry about it because you probably don't play these tones anyway.) The same can be said for any rock gig or church praise band situation. You don't want to wind up sounding like a lounge lizard at the wrong time. Definitely *do* feel free to add these complex tones at a jazz gig. (The more the merrier, unless it interferes with another band member's phrasing, or is contrary to the mood and melody of the tune.)

Stick close to the melody when performing for retirement homes, ship cruises, holiday parties, and of course sing-a-longs.* Stay away from extremely dissonant phrasing, comical quotes, or aggressive R&B licks at a funeral (*unless* the beloved's family specifically requests it). Enough said!

---

* I once got carried away jazzing up all my tunes at a Christmas party, thinking I was being very clever and creative, until the hostess came up to me and in an exasperated voice whined, "Honey, when *are* you going to play some Christmas music?!"

The I-vi-ii-V Progression

Idea #

Throughout music history, there've been special chord progressions commonly used by composers belonging to certain eras and cultures. The classical composers based their compositions largely upon the I, IV, and V chords (chords constructed on the root, fourth, and fifth tones of a major or minor scale). Modern music makes frequent use of the I–vi–ii–V progression. Naturally, these chords would be built on the root, sixth, second, and fifth tones of a scale, like so:

The Harmonized C Major Scale

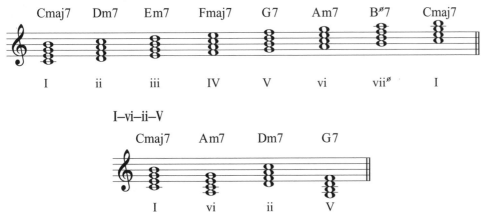

*Uppercase Roman numerals represent major chords; lowercase numerals represent minor chords.

If you've ever thumped out the bottom part to Hoagy Carmichael's "Heart and Soul," you should be familiar with the sound of a I–vi–ii–V progression. A large body of standards make use of it, including "Blue Moon" (Rodgers and Hart), "The Way You Look Tonight" (Jerome Kern), "At Last" (Harry Warren), "These Foolish Things" (Marvell, Link, and Strachey), "We're In This Love Together" (Murrah and Stegall), "Since I Fell For You" (Bud Johnson), "Stormy Weather" (Harold Arlen), "Sleigh Ride" (Leroy Anderson), "I Can't Get Started" (Vernon Duke), and "Polka Dots and Moonbeams" (Burke and Van Heusen), just to name a few. When George Gershwin came out with "I Got Rhythm" in 1930, its chords (mainly made up of I–vi–ii–V's) inspired a whole series of new tunes by Nat King Cole, Miles Davis, Duke Ellington, Charlie Parker, and a multitude of other musicians. These chords affected American music culture so much they even influenced cartoon themes and TV commercials!

A big benefit to improvising over the I–vi–ii–V progression is that you only need to remember the notes of the major scale based on the I chord (e.g., if you're improvising over a I–vi–ii–V progression in the key of C, play around with the notes from the C major scale).

This ever-popular progression is written out in the keys of C, G, and F for you to experiment with. Notice that the vi and the V chord are inverted for ease of playing in the left hand. In the right hand, improvise with the corresponding major scale for each key center:

TRACK 14

Key of C (C major scale)

play 6 times

TRACK 15

Key of G (G major scale)

play 6 times

TRACK 16

Key of F (F major scale)

play 6 times

Common Tones

The use of common tones in one hand while the harmony changes in the other can be very effective. *Common tones* (repeated notes that are in common with different chords or scales) can act as a basis to connect your phrases together. Many Brazilian tunes use common tones in their melodies, such as Antonio Carlos Jobim's "One-Note Samba," "Corcovado," and "Waters of March." These tunes get quite a bit of mileage out of one or two notes for many measures while the chords change frequently underneath.

Rock 'n' roll tunes typically use repeated melodic phrases. The blues is another form that makes great use of common tones. Duke Ellington's "C Jam Blues" is merely a two-note melody. Many other blues heads repeat the opening four-bar phrase three times, such as "Bag's Groove" by Milt Jackson, "Centerpiece" by Lambert, Hendricks, and Ross, as well as a large body of tunes by B.B. King. Hear the use of common tones in Ray Charles's hit "What'd I Say" and Chuck Berry's "Surfin' USA."

When a common tone is used in the bass line, it's called a *pedal point.* (This term originates from the practice of an organist planting a foot on a pedal and sustaining the bass note while the harmony is changing on the manual keyboards.) A pedal point is often based on the root or fifth of a key center. This device can really build excitement and tie a stream of chord changes together—plus it's an easy thing to do in the pianist's left hand because it's stationary! Tunes that incorporate pedal points are "On Green Dolphin Street" (N. Washington, B. Kaper), "Milestones" (Miles Davis), and the famous McCoy Tyner/John Coltrane version of "Body and Soul." The Sting version of the Ivan Lins tune "She Walks This Earth" has not only pedal points in the bass but also common tones throughout the chords.

Try some common tones in your arrangements and improvisations, and see what you think. Remember: a bit of repetition can be a good thing, but stop before it becomes a bore!

Thirds and Sixths

*Idea #*17

If you wish to add harmony to your right hand, it usually works best to put it *under* the melody. The melody will stand out the most if it's the very top voice. (Think of a choir. What section usually sings the melody? The sopranos, of course, because they have the highest voices!)

What tones are good to add under the melody? Chord tones are always a logical choice. Two other options that arrangers have been using for years are harmonizing with thirds and sixths. Here's how to do it.

Let's say you have the following melody to harmonize:

TRACK 17

Adding a third under this melody is easy. (A *third* is the distance of three scale tones.) If the melody is on a space, simultaneously write or play the note located on the next space below. If the melody is on a line, simply play the note the next line below.

Here's the same melody harmonized with thirds:

TRACK 17
cont'd

Adding the interval of a *sixth* (six scale tones apart) under the melody can also be a very pretty sound. To readily find a sixth, pretend you're reading bass clef. The first tone of this particular melody is an E in treble clef, but it is a G if you pretend it is in bass clef. Add a G under an E, and you get a sixth. Continue on in this manner.

Here is the same melody harmonized in sixths:

TRACK 17
cont'd

Certain situations may require you to "tweak" the thirds or sixths a bit depending on the harmony. Pay attention to the flats and sharps in the key center. If something doesn't quite sound right, try raising or lowering the bottom note one half step and see if that sounds better.

Harmonizing with Chord Tones

Idea # 18

As mentioned, another way to harmonize a RH melody is to add a few chord tones underneath. The notes you'd select depend on the harmonic structure of your piece. Grab two to three chord tones under the melody with the lower fingers in your right hand. Pay attention to what the chord symbols tell you.

Here's the previous melody phrased by adding basic chord tones:

TRACK 18

29

Spread Chords

Idea # 19

As a keyboardist, you already know that you can make a bigger sound by playing octaves in your RH instead of just a single-note melody. Jazz pianists like Red Garland, Erroll Garner, Oscar Peterson, Gene Harris, and others have amplified this idea with a technique known as *spread chords*. This particular technique imitates the "shout chorus" of a big-band piece, where all the horn players play a passage together for a strong, rich sound. When pianists play spread chords, both hands must use full harmonies and play every rhythm simultaneously.

To voice spread chords, start with an octave in the RH. Add a complementary chord tone in the middle of your RH—something you can easily grab with your second or third finger. Now for every note you play in your RH, back it up with a richly harmonized LH chord.* Use this technique when playing the melody to a tune in a piano trio setting, or at the high point of your solo. A chorus of spread chords goes a long way.

Once again, here is the same familiar melodic phrase, this time harmonized with spread chords:

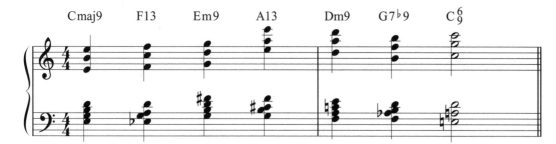

TRACK 19

* This example uses some rootless voicings. The implied roots would be supplied by the bass player.

Solo Voicings

Even if a keyboardist knows how to find the notes in a given chord, it can sometimes be a real challenge deciding how to arrange those tones between the two hands. Follow these basic guidelines for the best-sounding solo piano voicings:

- The melody must be on top.

- The root should usually be on the bottom (occasional inversions are okay).

- The remaining chord tones may be divided between the two hands.

Pianists are especially concerned about what to do with the left hand. One important thing to keep in mind is that notes close together at the bottom of the piano tend to sound muddy. Here are some suggestions for the LH with the lowest preferred range given. On a well-tuned piano, the left hand may play:

- Single notes, all the way down.

- Octaves, all the way down.

- A fifth, down to this F:

- A tenth chord, down to this B♭:

- A seventh (lowered), down to this F:

- Any closely voiced chord with thirds and seconds, down to this B♭:

Now just make sure the right hand has the melody on top and includes the missing chord tones. The right hand may also double some of the same chord tones if you wish.

Combo Voicings

Idea #

21

When playing in a jazz group with a bassist, you should treat the left hand differently. Playing roots and low bass notes is fine if you're in a rock or country band, but this practice is usually frowned upon in a jazz combo—especially by the bass player. In a jazz situation, bassists need room to improvise and substitute chords as they please, and they can't do that if the pianist is stepping all over their lines in the same low range. Ever since pianist Bill Evans started using inverted chords with his left hand up around middle C, this has been the way most jazz keyboardists choose to voice their chords.

Many jazz keyboardists build their chords starting with the third or the seventh on the bottom. This enables smooth voice leading from chord to chord with just two inversions. (Of course, the fifth on the bottom works fine too, but it's one more voicing to learn.) The LH needs to be near the middle C area to sound richest and clearest. The RH may be used to play the melody, improvise a solo, or *comp* (accompany) along with the LH. When a pianist comps, both hands should sound simultaneously to support the soloist. If the hands stagger, it draws too much attention to the keyboard and not the featured improviser—and everyone likes a moment in the spotlight!

Here are some suggested voicings for comping using a chord from the G7 family. These chords are built on the seventh and third in the LH, with the RH playing roots and fifths:

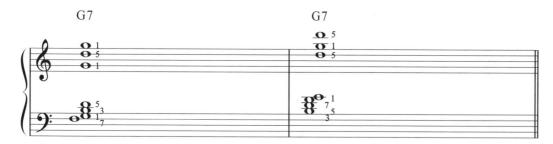

TRACK 20

Jazz pianists often add tones like ninths and thirteenths to their chords automatically. These upper chord extensions sound rich (and face it, jazzy!). They'll often add tones even if the fake book says to play a regular G7. To a jazz musician's ears, a plain old G7 sounds boring. Pianists often wonder how to play all the tones to these chords in just the left hand. The answer is... don't! The ninth replaces the root like this:

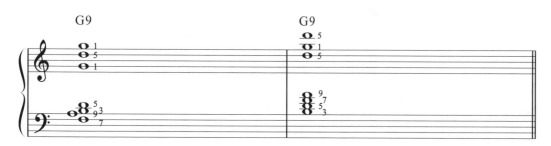

TRACK 20
cont'd

The 13th replaces the blandest chord tone, which is the fifth:

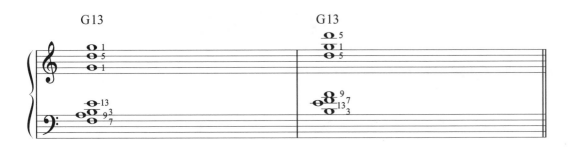

TRACK 20
cont'd

The 11th is perhaps the most startling chord tone to add. It has a lot of color and should be used sparingly for effect. For chords in the major family, the 11th is usually raised. Try including the sharp 11th in the RH as in the following polychord* voicings, which resemble A major triads in the RH over G9 chords in the LH:

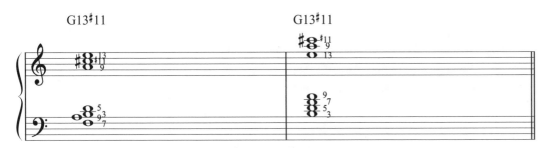

TRACK 20
cont'd

* A *polychord* resembles two different chords played simultaneously to form one new chord.

When Adding Extensions Doesn't Work

Idea #22

In certain circumstances, it will *not* be good to automatically add extensions. Be aware of the appropriateness of the musical situation (see idea #14). Keep your ears open when comping behind a soloist to make sure your voicings and harmonic styles don't clash. Also keep in mind the style and era of the tune.

That said, here are some guidelines for adding extensions:

- In general, ninths (the second scale tone) can be safely added to major sevenths, dominant sevenths, and most minor sevenths. Watch out when adding ninths to some iii7 chords because they may sound a bit odd. Not everyone's ears are ready for the strong sound of a ninth added to half diminished (m7♭5) or fully diminished seventh chords, so add cautiously.

- The natural eleventh (fourth tone) may be added to minor ninth chords. The raised eleventh, a very bright tone, may be added occasionally to major or dominant ninth chords.

- Thirteenths sound great when added to chords in the dominant family.

- Chords of the dominant family can support the most tension, and may often be changed with good-sounding results because they usually resolve to a more stable chord. Dominant chords can have *altered* (raised or lowered) fifths and/or ninths as long as these tones don't clash with the melody and style of the tune.

Quartal Chord Voicings
Idea #23

Traditionally, chords are formed by stacking thirds on top of one another. This is what's known as *tertian* harmony. These chord tones can then be *inverted* or rearranged in a different order for an array of voicings.

However, in the early 1960s, pianist McCoy Tyner popularized another way to voice chords, using *quartal* harmony. These chords are formed by stacking fourths instead of thirds. Since the '60s, pianists have been adding the bell-like quality of quartal chords to their palette of voicing colors.

Use quartal harmony for a more open, contemporary sound. The two voicings demonstrated below are from the G major or dominant family. They may be created by stacking fourths from the seventh or third up. However, you may find it easier to think of building these chords from the top note down. This G13 chord has the fifth tone (D) on top. Below the D is the interval of a fourth (A), under which is another fourth (E), followed by another fourth (B), ending with a lowered fourth (F):

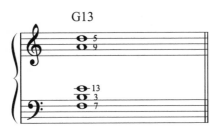

TRACK 21

This G6/9 chord is created by building fourths from the root down (G–D–A–E–B). The G6/9 chord can replace a G major triad or Gmaj7. In some cases, it can even replace a G dominant chord because of its open, noncommittal sound:

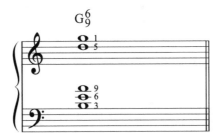

TRACK 21
cont'd

Sus Chords

Idea #

The sus chord is probably one of the most vague and confusing symbols you can encounter in music. There are various ways pianists interpret the sus chord depending on the situation. Each of the following symbols could be used to indicate a Dsus chord:

Dsus	**Dsus4**	**Dsus2**	**Dsus(2, 4)**	**D(add4, no 3rd) D4**
D(add9, no 3rd) D11		**D7sus**	**D7sus4**	**C/D** **Am7/D**

The list goes on. What's a keyboardist to do?

The word *sus* is short for *suspended*. In the good old days, this meant that the fourth tone of the scale was suspended (hung onto, keeping the listener in suspense) until it eventually resolved down to the third scale tone like the "amen" at the end of a hymn:

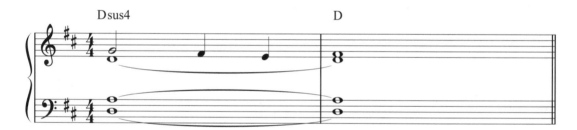

TRACK 22

These days, sus chords don't necessarily need to resolve as in the above example. Although music theorists may differ among themselves about exactly what tones are included in a sus chord, the general opinion is that it contains the fourth scale tone instead of the third. Beyond that, there are many extra tones you may add to a sus chord to suit your fancy.

Jazz pianist Herbie Hancock introduced us to a new way to use sus chords in his tune "Maiden Voyage." This tune's harmony consists entirely of four different sus chords, which have a very pretty, floating quality. Below are some examples of jazz-style sus chords. The first two are like polychords, while the last example uses quartal harmony:

TRACK 22
cont'd

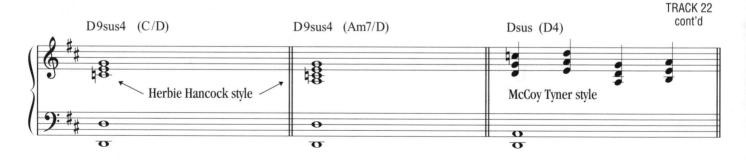

Jazz pianists often use the above voicings for sus chords. If you're working with a bass player, you can let the bassist play the root while you put the other tones of the chord in your left hand.

The pop music of today frequently uses not only the sus4 chord but also the sus2—sometimes both. The second is a nice tone to add to fill out a chord in a pop, folk, or church band situation where you don't want to sound too jazzy or clash with the guitarist:

TRACK 22
cont'd

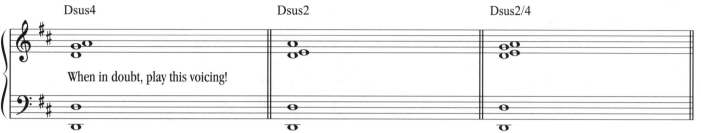

As you can tell, the symbol for a sus chord leaves a lot up to the performer. When in doubt, play a simple version of a sus4, and that should fit in just fine for most musical situations. For improvisation, use the Mixolydian scale, but emphasize the fourth scale tone, and avoid the third.

The Bass Line

Idea #

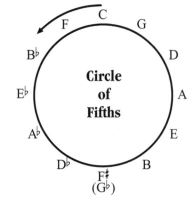

The real foundation for a tune's harmony is its bass line. A strong and well-phrased bass line will keep the music moving forward with energy. If the bass line is weak, the music will lack momentum and drive. Pianists and drummers know the importance of playing with a good, solid bassist. Although the average listener may be consciously focusing on only the melodic phrasing, they can sense on a physical or emotional level the bass line's contribution to the tune as a whole.

If you're playing solo piano, the bass line must be provided by your left hand if you want a full and complete-sounding arrangement. Be sure to have the roots on the bottom in your left hand at the start of *each new chord*. If each new chord does not contain the root as its lowest voice, it will sound like a wrong note, unless you're deliberately creating a pedal point or *substitution* (reharmonization). Before trying any chord substitutions, it's important to know how harmony tends to move:

1. Circle Movement

This is also known as moving down by fifths. If you observe a lot of standard tunes, you'll often find three roots in a row taken from this sequence:

C–F–B♭–E♭–A♭–D♭–G♭–B–E–A–D–G

2. Chromatic Movement

Bass lines commonly move chromatically (by half steps). Most often, a bass line will move *down* by half steps, but you do occasionally find upward lines, too.

It's common practice for jazz musicians to use a device called the *tritone substitution*. This device results in a chromatic line. Here's a brief explanation. Let's say you have the following common chord progression based on circle movement:

TRACK 23

Now replace the F7 chord with the dominant seventh chord three whole steps (a tritone) away. The replacement chord is B7:

TRACK 23
cont'd

The F7 and B7 chords can substitute so well for each other because they contain two common tones: the notes A and E♭ (D♯). Incidentally, these common tones are also a tritone apart from each other—another reason this device is called the tritone substitution!

You may wish to try this substitution when you run into dominant seventh chords in pieces.

3. Diatonic Movement

Diatonic movement means moving along a scale. Here are two possible examples:

C major: **Cmaj7–Dm7–Em7–Fmaj7**

C minor: **Cm7–Dm7–E♭maj7–Dm7**

For more about this, see idea #26.

4. Any Kind of Pattern

Consistent patterns work well for phrasing in the bass, including a series of whole steps, moving by major or minor thirds, etc.

Extra Chords

Idea #

26

Sometimes, you may wish to fill out your harmonic phrasing by adding extra chords. There are several things you can do to make the harmony less stagnant even if the tune says to stay on just one chord for two bars or longer. Here are a couple of ideas:

1) If you encounter a **major** chord that lasts for at least two bars, try diatonic movement. Move from the major chord up the scale until you reach the iii or IV chord and, if you have time, travel back down again:

TRACK 24

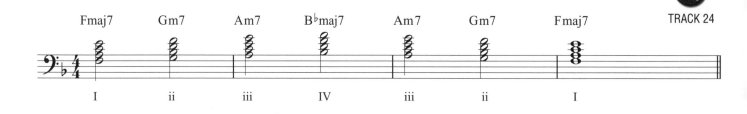

Try this device during the bridge to Billy Strayhorn's "Take the 'A' Train," or on the first few bars during the improvisation section to "Stompin' at the Savoy" (Sampson/Webb). The Bill Withers tune "Lean on Me" has this kind of movement already built in.

2) If you encounter a **minor** chord that lasts awhile, you can move the root down by half steps:

TRACK 24 cont'd

The following tunes each begin with a minor chord and take advantage of the above device: "A Song for You" and "This Masquerade" (Leon Russell), "My Funny Valentine" (Rodgers and Hart), "It Don't Mean a Thing" (Duke Ellington), "Puttin' On the Ritz" (Irving Berlin), and "What Are You Doing the Rest of Your Life" (Michel Legrand).

This same kind of movement makes a great salsa pattern, too:

TRACK 24 cont'd

Chromatic Side-Slipping

Idea # 27

Brief harmony that moves temporarily to the key either a half step above or below the main chord being played is known as *chromatic side-slipping* (or *side stepping*). The trick here is to move quickly up or down and return immediately to the main chord.

Let's say you were comping merrily along on an F7 chord and were starting to get bored. You could either slip quickly up to an F#7 and return to F7, or slip down to an E7 and return to F7. This makes a fun and useful comping device. When improvising in the right hand, you could continue phrasing your ideas based on the F7 harmony, or move your RH ideas to match the temporary keys of F# or E.

TRACK 25

Certain tunes have chromatic side-slipping automatically built in. Check out the bridge to "Stompin' at the Savoy" by Edgar Sampson/Chick Webb and the opening eight bars to Thelonious Monk's "Well You Needn't." Some other tunes such as "Just In Time" (Styne) and the bridge to "Sentimental Journey" (Green/Brown/Homer) have chromatic side-slipping built into the melody but not the harmony. In these types of tunes, it may sound good to support the chromatic movement in the melody with complementary chromatic chords in the left hand. Experiment with this technique, and see what you think.

Chromatic Passing Chords

Idea #28

Another related idea to try is using chromatic passing chords. If the roots of two consecutive chords are a minor third apart, and you have enough time in the music to do so, try slipping up or down by half steps between the two chords.

You may wish to try this device with a tune like "Sweet Georgia Brown" (Bernie/Pinkard/Casey). This tune, when written in the key of F, moves down a minor third to a D7 chord in the first bar. Before playing the D7, slide F7–E7–E♭7, then arrive at D7. This device also works well in many bridges to standard tunes where the chords sometimes move down by minor thirds, such as Fats Waller's "Honeysuckle Rose."

TRACK 26

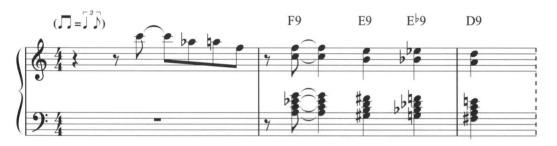

Apply the same technique if the chords move up a minor third, such as Am to Cm (play Am–B♭m–Bm–Cm). There are opportunities to try this out during "The Shadow of Your Smile" (Johnny Mandel) and "Save Your Love for Me" (Buddy Johnson).

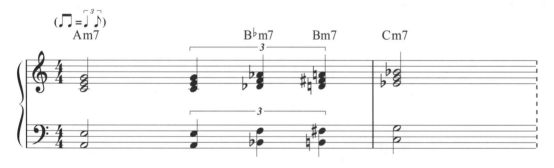

When improvising over chromatic chord changes, often the best-sounding solution is to arpeggiate the chord tones. In the case where a tune is pretty well grounded in a certain key center for a while, such as "Autumn Leaves" (Mercer/Prevert), you may continue improvising with the key center scale if the chromatic chords move very quickly and last a short duration.

Chromatic Pickups

Idea # 29

Chromatic chords may also be used effectively to harmonize in contrary motion underneath an ascending melodic phrase. This device works especially well when you want to harmonize *pickup notes* (notes before the first complete measure of a tune).

The following is an example of three pickup notes that arpeggiate a major seventh chord.* Notice that these notes lead up to the first chord of this example, Fmaj7:

TRACK 27

Think of the Fmaj7 as your *target chord,* or the chord that you're aiming for. Now the fun part begins! Count the number of notes in the melody before this target chord. (Three, right?) Next, count up three half steps above your target chord's root. (You should arrive at the note A♭.) Your contrary motion bass line will start with A♭ and move chromatically downward until you arrive at the Fmaj7 chord on beat 1.

Experiment with different chord qualities and voicings until you're satisfied with your newly harmonized, contrary-motion pickup notes. Ask yourself, "What relationship is this melody note to the bass, and what kind of chord can I make with these notes?" The first melody tone is F; the first bass note is A♭. The first chord made with these notes could be an A♭6, A♭13, A♭m6, D♭/A♭, or many other possibilities. Be creative and have fun! This next example shows one way to harmonize this:

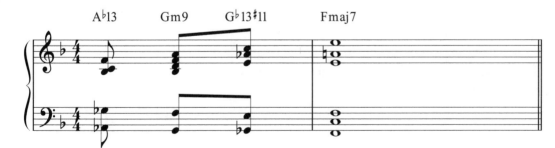

TRACK 27
cont'd

* This opening melodic phrase is similar to what appears in the following tunes: "I Can't Get Started" (Vernon Duke), "I Loves You Porgy" (Gershwin), "Samba de Orpheo" (Bonfa), and "I Thought About You" (Mercer/Van Heusen), although in the last tune these notes are actually in the first complete measure.

Now let's try harmonizing an even longer ascending melodic phrase. Observe the following series of six notes with a target chord of Dm11, similar to the opening phrase of Duke Ellington's beautiful ballad "In a Sentimental Mood":

TRACK 27
cont'd

Counting six half steps above D, we arrive at the note A♭. The following example is just one way to fill in the chord tones between the ascending melody and descending chromatic bass line:

TRACK 27
cont'd

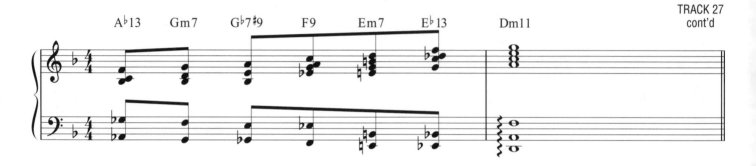

How about trying this exercise with a different target chord? What if the same series of notes led into a Bm7♭5, as though we were going to start Gershwin's tune "Someone to Watch Over Me"? Try this example:

TRACK 27
cont'd

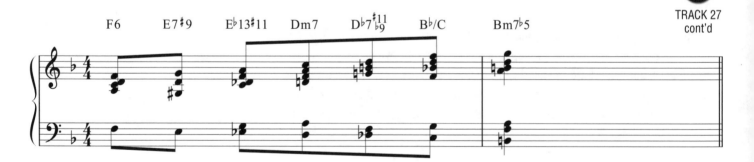

When harmonizing with all these rich, additional chords, be sure to choose appropriate tunes played slowly—both for ease of performance and to allow time for the listener to absorb all of the sophisticated musical colors!

The Swing Thing

Idea # 30

Duke Ellington wrote a tune called "It Don't Mean a Thing If It Ain't Got That Swing." What is a swing feel, and how do you get your brain and fingers to do it?

Swing can be a very subtle way of phrasing that gives music its toe-tapping drive. It cannot be written out precisely and cannot be forced. Swing must have a natural flow. There are certain techniques a pianist can do to help the fingers swing, but first you must hear it in your head. Listening over and over to players that swing well (like pianists Gene Harris and Oscar Peterson) is the first and most important step.

You can assume that most jazz should be played with swinging eighth notes, unless otherwise indicated. Swing feels are sometimes written out with even eighth notes, but if you played the following as written it would sound very stiff:

TRACK 28

Occasionally, a writer will indicate a swing feel using *dotted eighths* and *sixteenths:*

TRACK 28
cont'd

However, a swing feel most closely approximates this triplet notation, which is rarely used because it looks so confusing:

TRACK 28
cont'd

One compromise is to notate swing with even eighth notes but add a special indication at the beginning of the piece (♫ = ♩♪) telling you to play each eighth-note pair as if it were a quarter-eighth triplet. (This is the method used for the excerpts in this book.)

The following styles of music use *even* eighth notes and should not be swung:

- Brazilian
- Latin/salsa
- Rock (some, but not all)
- Funk
- Fusion
- Ballads (some, but not all)
- Very fast jazz
- New age

Laying Back

Idea # 31

To create a natural-sounding swing feel, it's important to relax. Jazz musicians call playing slightly behind the beat *laying back*. It's true that improvisation is exhilarating and can get a musician all pumped up, but you want to sound relaxed and in the groove to swing!

First of all, get your technique down well enough so that it won't hinder your ideas. This means knowing your chords, scales, and comfortable fingerings, which are essential to getting around the keyboard with ease. Try using grace notes and dragging your fingers from black to white keys to help slow yourself down. If you can find a bassist and drummer who swing well, practice deliberately laying back while they keep a steady groove. A second choice would be to work out with a drum machine or metronome and let it keep time while you play slightly behind. Don't be lured into sounding robotic along with these machines.

The best instrument to practice this technique on is a real piano. Keyboards, even with weighted keys, just don't respond the way an acoustic piano does. If your main instrument is the organ and you don't play piano at all, try practicing as close to your speakers (or pipes!) as possible so you won't be playing ahead of the beat to compensate for the delay in time it takes the sound to reach your ears.

Scale Accents

Idea #

32

Often when aspiring pianists first try to swing, they overdo it. By trying to force the swing feel out of their fingers, it comes out sounding more like dotted eighths and sixteenths. Before you give up or decide to apply for a job recording elevator music, keep on reading.

The swing feel sounds laid back but also contains certain accents. In order to create and control these accents, try the following scale exercises. Pick any scales you want. Play them rhythmically even, but accent every other note. Play each scale at least two octaves up and down:

TRACK 29

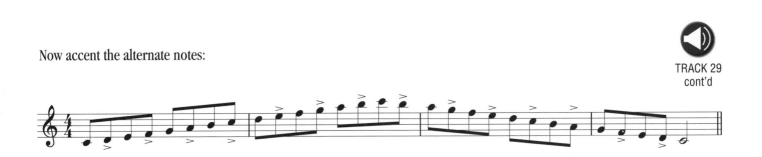

Now accent the alternate notes:

TRACK 29
cont'd

Practice several scales each day for two weeks. After practicing scales this way, you'll have a more natural swing sound.

Accents within Phrases

Idea # 33

When trying to create phrases that swing, stay away from thinking "doot-dah, doot-dah, doot." Doing so will make you sound marchlike or corny. Instead, think of this more legato-sounding "doo-bah, doo-bah, doo-bah."

Most of the notes combined within a phrase should be legato, with the exception of repeated notes, ends of phrases, and accented staccato offbeats (notes that don't fall on beats 1, 2, 3, or 4, but between). You will want to draw attention to offbeats by really nailing them with a heavily accented "bop"—especially when playing jazz, Brazilian, and Afro-Cuban or salsa music, which all contain lots of offbeats.

The tops of phrases are other good points to accent. If a musical phrase were written out like a graph, the high points or peaks would be the desirable places to accent:

TRACK 30

Here is the phrase in musical notation:

Rhythmic Displacement

Idea #
34

Another intriguing idea to play with is *rhythmic displacement.* This simply means playing around with the rhythms of a phrase. A pianist can use the same notes or even the same rhythms and start them on a different beat in the bar for an effect. This example uses just the notes C, G, and B:

TRACK 31

Rhythmic displacement is used effectively during the "I know, I know, I know..." part to Bill Withers's "Ain't No Sunshine." For additional examples, check out Luis Bonfa's "Une Barquino" (also known as "My Little Boat") and Thelonious Monk's "Straight No Chaser."

Left-Hand Rhythms

Idea #

35

When pianists first start dabbling in improvisation, they're often puzzled by what to do rhythmically with the left hand. After all, they have so many things to think about: voicings for the LH, note choices for the RH, and most importantly, how to keep their place in the tune while improvising and fitting in with other players in the band. Since all of these things can be overwhelming, novice improvisers usually try to keep their place in the music by comping on the first beat of every bar. However, once a pianist begins to feel a certain degree of confidence with his or her sense of time, it's good to explore other options for when to play the LH. We'll explore those options now, but keep in mind that the end result will be something a pianist *feels* almost subconsciously.

1. **Play the LH in between the RH.**

   Think of your two hands as having a conversation. The RH is the talkative person, making different length phrases. The LH interjects little comments like, "Yeah. Uh huh. Right."

   TRACK 32

2. **Play the LH mostly in between the RH.**

   Occasionally, strike the LH simultaneously with the RH to create an accent:

   TRACK 32
   cont'd

3. Play both hands simultaneously.

This results in a "spread chord" effect (see idea #19).

TRACK 32
cont'd

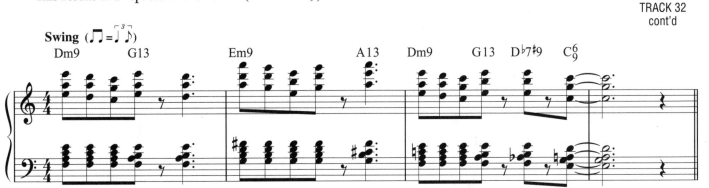

4. Use a consistent pattern in the LH.

Not too many pianists use this idea because it's actually harder than it sounds. The challenge is to sound loose and free in the RH while pulling off the coordination of a consistent rhythm in the LH. Two pianists who made this technique sound easy were Red Garland (with a light "Charleston"-type LH) and Erroll Garner (a guitar-like strum):

TRACK 32
cont'd

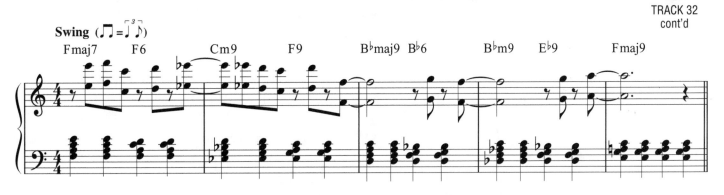

Troubleshooting

Idea #

36

Q: Help! Everything I do sounds the same and boring.

A: Congratulations! You are now ready to move up to the next level.

When you first got into improvising, your mind was probably racing trying to keep a kazillion facts straight about chord tones, voicings, scale choices, melodic ideas, the feel of the tune, and keeping your place. Now it sounds as though you have your tools together and you are beyond nervous—you're bored.

Usually when people say their ideas "sound the same," it's because they've gotten stuck in a rhythmic rut. Believe it or not, the best way to break out of this rut is to pick just a few notes to improvise with, and concentrate on a variety of creative rhythmic ways to play these notes. Solo over the C blues using just the note G, and see how many rhythms you can do. Next time, add one more note (perhaps C) and play with just those two notes. The end result will be rhythmic inspiration.

Here are some other things to try:

- *Different phrase lengths.* Think of improvisation as telling a story, with sentences of various lengths.

- *Play the left hand on different beats.* This will help vary the phrase lengths.

- *Start your phrases on different beats.* To get out of a rut, practice starting all your phrases on beat 1, then beat 2, then 3, then 4, then the offbeats.

Q: I recently got together with a band to jam and found that I had rhythm problems. What can I do to improve my time?

A: Tempo problems, either rushing or dragging, usually arise from inexperience and/or insecurity. If you can tell that you need help, there is hope! (It's the person who has no clue he has a rhythm problem who's hard to fix.)

It is a fact that rhythmic mistakes get noticed more than melodic ones. The keyboard player who has trouble with time will find it difficult to get other musicians to work with him or her. Here are some solutions.

If you tend to add a beat or drag:

- Learn to make more fluent transitions between chords.

- Become more comfortable with the melody and scales.

- Don't think back about how weird the last note sounded.

- Take the tempo slower, and play more simply.

If you tend to drop a beat or rush:

- Calm down!

- Count carefully, and practice with a metronome. (Use one with a beeper or accent on beat 1.)

- Don't try to be complex until you get your timing together.

- If you're playing in a group, get your own part together so you can listen to the bass and drums.

Q: I would love to be able to play fast when I improvise. I can play classical music allegro, but when I improvise I can only do simple, short phrases. Why is this?

A: I used to wonder why I could play classical music at breakneck speed, yet I could only improvise *andante*. I was very envious of the players who would blow people away with their impressive flying fingers. It finally dawned on me that with classical music I would practice the same passage over and over until my hand naturally and quickly found the notes, but when I was improvising I was trying to play new notes rapidly. My brain would send my hand a message, "Play fast!" and my hand would ask my brain, "Play what?" Then there would be a lag in time where my brain and fingers were fighting each other, and I'd lose the beat and sound stupid.

The following exercise will solve this problem and keep your fingers moving while developing a solid sense of rhythmic articulation. It sounds very strange, but it really works! Take your metronome and set it to a speed where you can *comfortably* play a steady stream of even eighth notes. I call this *noodling*: It doesn't matter what notes you play in the RH, just keep the notes steadily wandering all over the keyboard in time. If you hesitate or miss a note, slow down the tempo until it's nice and easy. Your brain shouldn't be consciously directing your fingers unless they get stuck in one area. Let the rhythm flow!

Each day, gradually increase the tempo one notch until the metronome won't go any faster with eighth notes. Then go back to your starting tempo and use triplets. Eventually work up to sixteenths. Do this one minute per day.

Crazy Lyrics

Complex rhythms, even when they're written out on the chart right in front of you, are sometimes hard to articulate with the proper inflection and feel. This is where the "crazy lyric" idea comes in handy.

Once when I was rehearsing on the harpsichord with my high school orchestra, the conductor did a very strange thing that has permanently stuck with me. It was getting close to performance time, and the string section was just not getting the rhythm to the Vivaldi piece we were playing. Mr. Harvey threw down his baton and yelled, "Look, kids, it's simple. Think: *Um! Ba-na-na fruit-cake. Um! Ba-na-na fruit-cake.*"

Immediately everyone caught on, and the rhythm was a "piece of cake" (rimshot).

Jazz rhythms may be particularly hard to interpret. The above approach can be applied to phrasing bebop and other kinds of complex rhythms. In fact, the name *bebop* came from the rhythm the jazz musicians often ended their phrases with. Say the name out loud to Dizzy Gillespie's tune "Oop Bop Sh-bam, A Cooglemop," and you'll naturally be speaking the correct rhythm of that tune.

Crazy lyrics may be nonsense syllables or real words—whatever helps get the phrasing right. A standard tune that seems to give a lot of people trouble during the opening rhythm is John Lewis's "Afternoon in Paris." The rhythm resembles this:

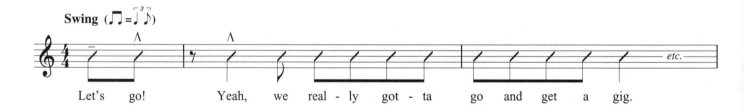

If you think of the phrase, "Let's go! Yeah—we really gotta go and get a gig," it just might help with the proper rhythmic inflections.

Try coming up with your own crazy lyrics to difficult rhythms and see if it helps you catch on to them faster.

Working with Singers

Idea # 38

Chances are very good that if you play keyboard you'll at some point be backing up a singer. Perhaps *you* are that singer. Phrasing well with singers takes a certain kind of skill and talent. The pianist has to be a good support, interacting intuitively and creatively with the vocalist while the singer interacts with the audience.

As an accompanist, you have to understand the singer's own particular way of phrasing. Does the singer want you to keep tempo while they lay back or play around with the phrasing of a tune? Do they want you to keep a rock steady support, or follow them as they speed up and slow down? Do they have a great sense of time, or need you to do something obvious to keep them on track? Are they strong minded or easily swayed? Do they like to count off a tune, or expect you to suggest the tempo? How does the singer typically end a tune? Do they give obvious physical cues, subtle ones, or depend on you to take charge?

Be sure to always provide an intro, unless the singer has another way of obtaining the first pitch. The last four bars of any song make an excellent intro in most cases. Listen to how the singer breathes for subtle cues about when to do an appropriate fill, and watch their body language especially at the endings. Maintain eye contact at the beginning of the tune, and especially after the instrumentalists are through improvising to let the singer know you are ready for him or her to come back in. Make sure the top note of your chord voicing doesn't clash with the singer's pitch. (Avoid voicing a half step away from the melody.)

Listen to the wonderful interactions between singer Tony Bennett and pianist Ralph Sharon, Mel Torme and George Shearing, and Ella Fitzgerald and Tommy Flanagan. The "king" of backing up his own vocals at the piano was none other than Nat King Cole. He had the gift for supplying perfect pianistic phrases, impeccably timed to complement his warm vocals. (Later in his career, Nat actually preferred to stand up and sing while someone else backed him at the piano because he felt it freed him up vocally. I personally feel the pianists of the world experienced a great loss when he did this!) Pianist/singer Diana Krall has paid tribute to the Nat King Cole Trio sound by modeling her instrumentation after him: a pianist who sings, backed by guitar and bass. She trades off accompanying her vocals with the guitar.

Working with Guitarists

Idea #39

The guitar and the piano have a lot in common: Both instruments are melodic, harmonic, and percussive. Because of this, when they get together, they can either be mutually supportive or drive each other crazy. It can be an advantage for both the guitarist and pianist to be freed from constant comping duties if they allow this to be an opportunity to try other musical ideas.

In order for a guitar and keyboard to work together in a band, both players must listen extremely well and, at times, compromise. Both instrumentalists need to agree in advance upon any extra chords or substitutions—unless the players have amazing ears or are psychically in tune with one another!

Here are some basic strategies to consider and discuss with the guitarist:

- **One instrument is predominant; the other fits in**. If the guitarist is the bandleader, let him or her take the main fills, play louder, do most of the comping, be the first to solo, etc., while you work around. Of course, the guitarist needs to fit around you if you are in charge.

TRACK 33

- **One instrument plays more rhythmically; the other plays sustained**. The guitarist can do a dry, percussive sound, while the pianist does sustained chords or arpeggios. A keyboardist can do string pads or different washes of smooth instrumental colors.

TRACK 33
cont'd

- **One instrument plays in a higher register; the other plays lower**. Both instruments most naturally tend to comp in the midrange, and this can lead to a thick and heavy sound. Pianists may opt to play at the outer extremes of their instrument in the same way Count Basie did with his band.

TRACK 33
cont'd

- **One instrument plays a predictable pattern; the other works around it**. In the Basie band, guitarist Freddie Green strummed four-to-the-bar in quarter notes while the Count worked around Freddie's pattern.

TRACK 33
cont'd

- **One instrument thins out the chords while the other plays fuller voicings**. Two good tones to play from a chord are the third and seventh. The other instrumentalist can then add extensions if they choose.

TRACK 33
cont'd

- **One instrument comps while the other plays a line**. The guitarist can provide a smooth line that harmonizes while the pianist comps, or the guitarist can comp while the pianist improvises a line an octave or two apart.

TRACK 33
cont'd

- **Take turns!** This should be an obvious solution, but few musicians think of it. Decide who comps under the sax solo, who plays fills, who backs up the singer, etc. Then when it's time, lay out! (That means don't play. Take a break.)

TRACK 33
cont'd

The pianist and guitarist should also discuss how much comping they want under their own solos. Different musicians have different preferences. Communication is the key!

Working without a Bassist

Whenever you're playing in situations without a bassist, you must do things in the left hand to compensate. If you're working with a singer or horn player, it's not necessary to provide the melody, but you do need to be concerned about providing the bass part and chords. Be sure that most of your two-handed voicings contain roots on the bottom; otherwise, the harmony will sound empty (see idea #20). Another idea is to comp the chords with your RH while providing some kind of LH device that keeps the rhythm going.

The following examples of how to construct a *walking bass line* will come in handy when you find yourself at a bassless gig. Listen to recordings of Dave McKenna to hear a top-notch pianist at this style. The purpose of the walking bass line is to imitate an upright or electric bass player. Walking bass is a more modern device for the LH than swing bass or boogie-woogie and can certainly come in handy during these times when clubs are cutting back on money for multiple band members—often, the keyboard player alone has to sound like a five-piece band!

There are two main rules for this type of bass line:

Rule #1:   **Keep a steady beat using mostly quarter notes.**

Rule #2:   **Always play the root first under any new chord.**

Below are some sample bass lines, from simple to more complex. Each line follows the same chord progression: Dm7–G7–C6–Em7/A7. Comp the chords in your RH while playing each line in your LH.

TRACK 34

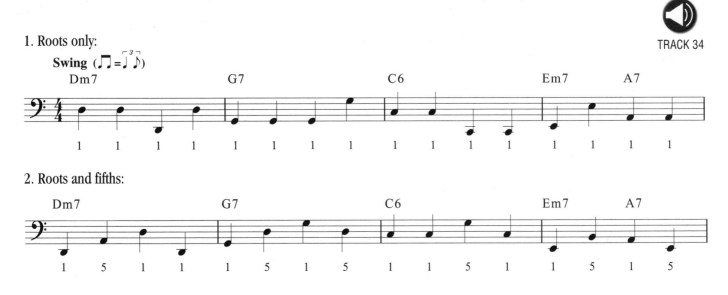

3. Arpeggiating up:

4. Arpeggiating down:

5. Arpeggiating combinations:

6. Scale tones:

7. Chromaticism:

Bass players typically use a combination of all these. A good bass line has a balance between upward and downward movement without being predictable. It should cover a range of about 1 1/2 to 2 1/2 octaves and may go as low on the piano as you deem tasteful. But *never* use the sustain pedal with this device!

Playing for Dancers

Idea #

41

Playing for dancers can be a whole different ballroom game. If you're at a lounge gig, and a couple who look as though they've only had two lessons at the local Arthur Murray Studio hit the floor, you may need to rein in your ideas and play very simply and squarely. Skip the polyrhythms, complicated ideas, and bass solos. If they request a waltz, forget phrasing like Bill Evans, and keep it to a basic "ONE-two-three" beat.

The only exception to the above advice would be if the dancers really looked like they knew their stuff. If experienced dancers come up to the bandstand and say something like, "Give me an up-tempo swing beat at 240," this would be your cue to be creative and enjoy the experience. Dancers and musicians can greatly influence each other, both positively and negatively. If the dancers look really bad, don't watch!

Classical (Theme and Variations)

Idea # 42

Imagine the following scenario… It's a Saturday afternoon, almost time for the wedding gig. You rush to the chapel just in time to begin playing, only to discover that the keyboard you're to play is an old pipe organ, located in the balcony up a musty flight of winding stairs. It's positioned in such a way that you cannot possibly see the wedding party coming down the aisle (unless you crane your neck completely around), and a relative of the bride has just informed you that there's been a change in plans: They want you to play Pachelbel's "Canon in D" not only for the bridesmaids, but also for the candle lighters and mothers and grandparents of the wedding couple.

If you're a musician who reads strictly by the notes, you could be in big trouble. The six-page sheet music version of this tune may either be too long (whereby the wedding party may be standing at the altar for an eternity until you finish playing) or, even worse, too short (if the music stops with the bride stuck halfway down the aisle). But here's a solution for you: Realize that the Pachelbel "Canon in D" is simply the following easily memorized four-bar chord progression played over and over, with variations:

To imitate classical phrasing, use patterns (think "theme and variations"). Take one idea, try it with the first chord, and then repeat the same technique for the rest of the chords in the above progression. In the case of classical phrasing, sequential ideas will sound best. Techniques that work well for this style: harmonizing by thirds under the melody, playing with arpeggios or broken chords, and inverting the chords in both the right and left hands, singularly and together. Experiment with half- or whole-measure patterns based on the D major scale. Play with different note values, choosing everything from half notes to sixteenths. Make your variations as long or short as necessary. Don't forget to start slowly and build your ideas utilizing range, texture, and volume!

TRACK 35

Rock

Idea # **43**

The next series of grooves are for comping and improvisation practice. Listen to each one first, then remove the recorded piano part and replace it with your own. Some scale suggestions are listed, but ultimately use whatever works for you. A few keyboardists who excel in each style are listed for inspiration.

This first track is a rock groove based on a C minor blues progression. Improvise with even eighth notes. The C blues scale will work well throughout.

Form

Comp: *2 times*

Improvise: *2 times*

TRACK 36

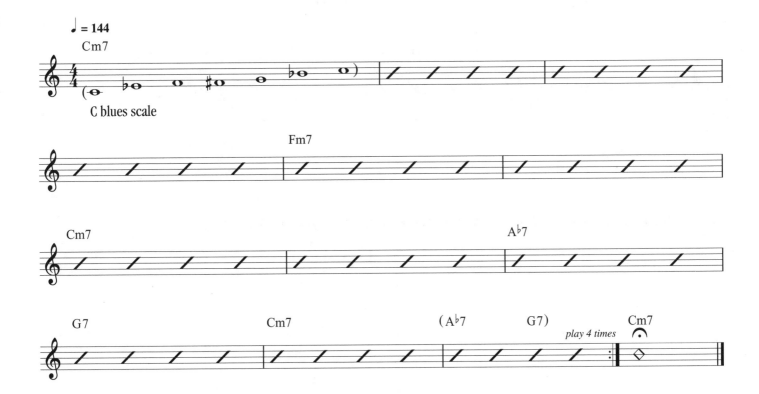

Suggested artists: Keith Emerson, Elton John, Billy Joel, Carole King, and Tori Amos.

Bossa Nova

This gentle Brazilian beat uses even eighth notes and has lots of syncopation. Solo using chord tones and notes chosen from the corresponding suggested scales.

Form

> **Comp:** *2 times*
>
> **Improvise:** *2 times*

TRACK 37

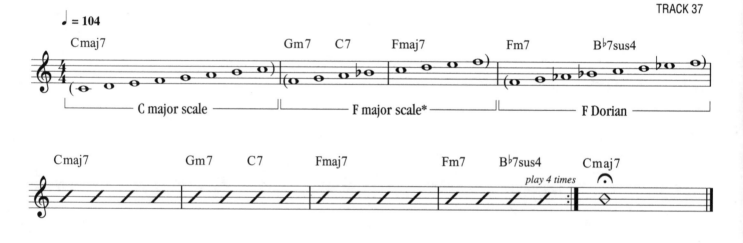

* G Dorian = C Mixolydian = F major

Suggested artists: Tania Maria, Eliane Elias, Antonio Carlos Jobim, and Antonio Adolfo.

Salsa/Afro-Cuban

Idea #

45

You may wish to add extensions to these chords, or keep them as pure triads. Try improvising in double octaves or in tenths. One hand can arpeggiate a chord while the other hand plays the next inversion away like this:

Notice above that the LH is arpeggiating in root position while the RH is using first inversion.

Form

Comp: *4 times*

Improvise: *4 times*

TRACK 38
cont'd

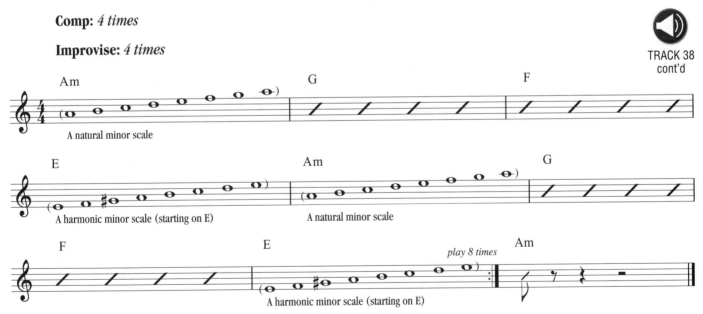

Suggested artists: Michel Camilo, Eddie Palmieri, Ruben Gonzales, Chucho Valdés, Danilo Perez, and Gonzalo Rubalcaba.

Ballad

Idea # 46

Ballad tempos can range from excruciatingly slow to mild swing. They can be slightly out of time (rubato), played with even eighth notes, or have a tripletlike feel, as in a 12/8 ballad. The following I–vi–ii–V chord progression is used in many ballads. Sometimes, you'll hear slight variations of the chord qualities. Listen to the feel on the next example, and fit in with the mood. The C major scale will work over all four chords.

Form

Comp: *4 times*

Improvise: *4 times*

TRACK 39

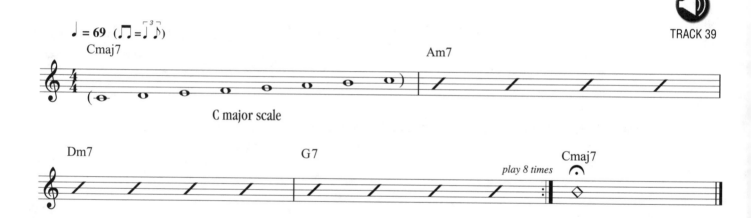

Suggested artists: Bill Evans, Marian McPartland, Hank Jones, George Shearing, Bill Mays, Sir Roland Hanna, and Roger Kellaway.

Jazz Waltz

The jazz waltz is not your danceable "oom-pah-pah" feel. It's rhythmically more complex and does not emphasize beat 1 in such an obvious way. Listen to the next pattern and then play along.

Form

    Comp: *4 times*

    Improvise: *4 times*

TRACK 40

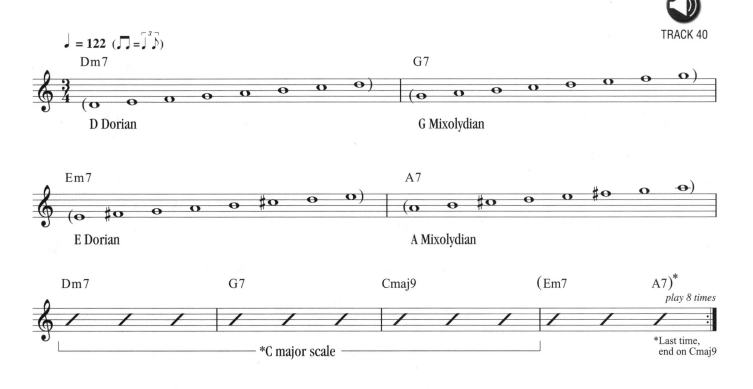

* D Dorian, G Mixolydian, and C major all use the same notes.

Suggested artists: Bill Evans, Vince Guaraldi, and Dave Brubeck (who excelled in playing odd time signatures).

Slow and Bluesy

Idea #48

This example uses I7–VI7–II7–V7 with all dominant seventh chords. Both the G and the E blues scale will work well for this sound.

Form

Comp: *4 times*

Improvise: *4 times*

TRACK 41

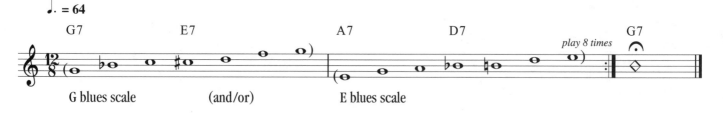

Suggested artists: Gene Harris, Dr. John, Ray Charles, Ramsey Lewis, and Jimmy Smith.

Swing

Idea #

49

Here's a swing groove based on a C blues progression. Improvise using the C blues scale or the A blues scale.

Form

Comp: *2 times*

Improvise: *2 times*

TRACK 42

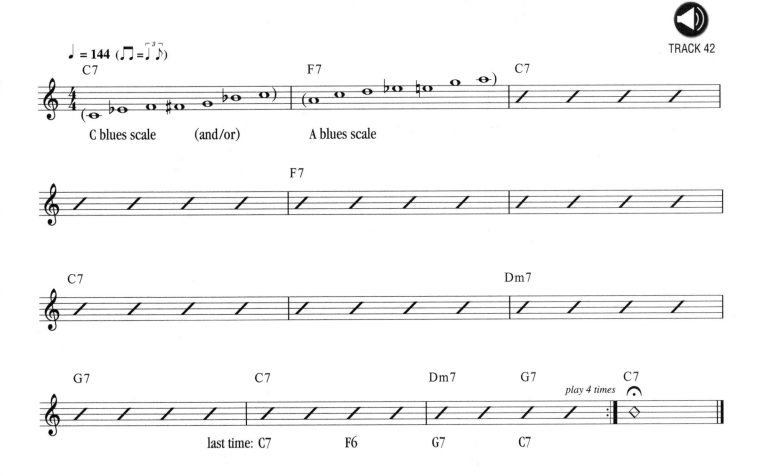

Suggested artists: Oscar Peterson, Nat King Cole, Teddy Wilson, Count Basie, Red Garland, Mary Lou Williams, and Duke Ellington.

Up-Tempo Jazz and Bebop

Idea #

50

This last groove is based on the same chord progression that George Gershwin used when he wrote his influential tune "I Got Rhythm." Jazz musicians call these chords "rhythm changes." Along with the blues, this is an important set of chords to know for jam sessions and jazz gigs.

Before attempting *any* tune at a fast tempo, it's important to warm up first. Play the "noodling exercise" explained in idea #36. Practice the arpeggio exercises (idea #2) over rhythm changes. Although it may sound like a contradiction, you need to prepare for rapid tempos by practicing very s-l-o-w-l-y—to allow yourself enough time to think. In addition to very slow practice, try practicing the piece a notch or two *faster* than the tempo indicates. This way, you can relax a bit when you perform the tune at full speed because it won't seem impossibly fast anymore.

The suggested scales will work well over basic rhythm changes. However, the easiest phrases to pull off at rapid tempos are ones that lie comfortably under your hand without a lot of crossing over and leaping around. Try playing short repeated figures with clever timing and well-placed accents. If you let the rest of the rhythm section "cook" underneath you, they'll make you sound like you're flying over the tune! You won't need to comp every chord indicated when playing at fast tempos, either. One comp per bar is plenty. (Accomplished jazz musicians may play a whole array of substitutions for these chords with a multitude of additional scales to match!) Notice the use of the I–vi–ii–V progression in this form.

Form

Comp: *1 time*

Improvise: *1 time*

TRACK 43

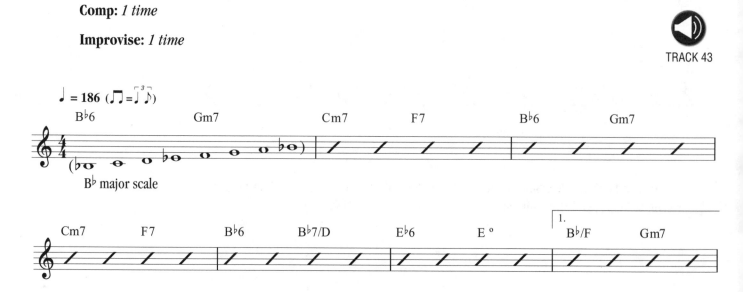

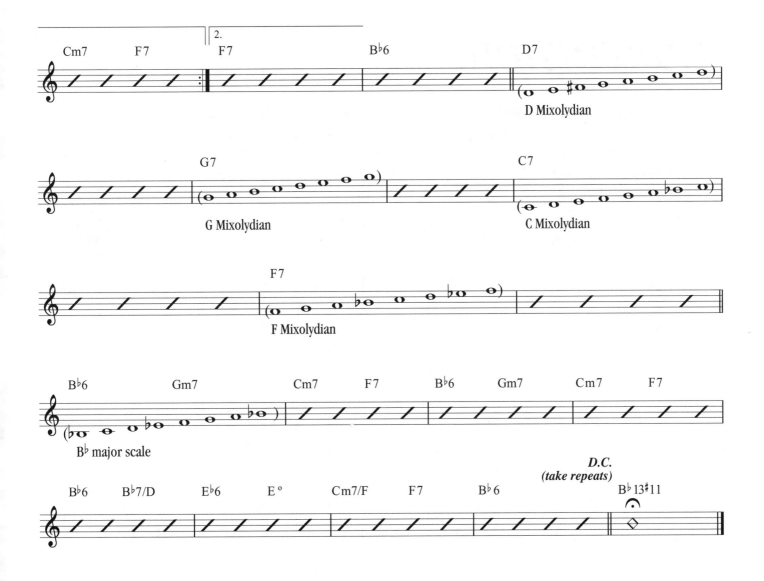

Suggested artists: Bud Powell, Thelonious Monk, Duke Jordan, John Lewis, and Billy Taylor.

Here's a partial list of tunes based on "rhythm changes":

Sonny Rollins	"Oleo"
Miles Davis	"The Theme"
Thelonious Monk	"Rhythm-A-Ning"
Lester Young	"Lester Leaps In"
Charlie Parker	"Moose the Mooch" and "Anthropology"
Nat King Cole	"Straighten Up and Fly Right" and "I'm an Errand Boy for Rhythm"
Duke Ellington	"Cotton Tail"
Billy Taylor	"One for the Woofer"
Bryson/Goldberg	"The Flinstone Theme"
Jon Hendricks	"Cloudburst"

Conclusion

Now that you've made it through to the end of this book, go back to CD track 3 and play along to hear just how much your phrasing has improved. These *Amazing Phrasing* ideas should get you started on a creative musical journey, and most importantly show you how to have fun phrasing things your very *own* way!

The CD concludes with track 44, another take on "Amazing Grace," this time played by a four-piece jazz combo: bass, drums, piano, and sax.

TRACK 44

About the Author

Debbie Denke has been teaching improvisation for nearly twenty years. Her background is in classical piano. With both a BA and MA in piano performance from the University of California at Santa Barbara, Ms. Denke has worked professionally as a jazz pianist, dance accompanist, church organist, composer, singer, and bandleader. She currently keeps a full schedule performing in concerts and clubs in Southern California. She teaches both privately and at Santa Barbara City College.

Debbie Denke is the author of *The Aspiring Jazz Pianist* book/CD, published by Hal Leonard Corporation. She lives in Santa Barbara with her husband Kim Collins and their daughters Melody and Madeline.

Acknowledgments

Kim: I wish to thank you most of all for the many hats you wear and for all you have done for this project—especially your musical, technical, editorial, and parental contributions. You are brilliant! **Jon, Joe, and Paul:** You are amazing musicians and a real joy to make phrases with. You guys did such a great job setting up those various little eight-bar grooves, I only wish we could have kept playing and recording music for a month straight! **Emmet:** You are truly gifted and such a gentle genius. Thanks for recording us. **Cheryl and Jim Gilinger:** You helped make this project go smoothly and offered good advice. **Gene Lees:** I enjoy our musical discussions immensely and you have given me insights about ideas to include. **Mom:** Thanks for all of the prayers and support! (Dad's inspiration is felt throughout this book.)

Last of all, thanks to my piano students for your endless questions, suggestions, and enthusiasm. This book is dedicated to you.

Musicians

Debbie Denke: piano and keyboard
Kim Collins: acoustic bass, electric bass, and vocals
Joe Dougherty: drums
Jon Crosse: flute, tenor and alto saxophones
Paul Murphy: guitars

Solo piano recorded at Cliffdwellers, Santa Barbara
Group recorded at Beagle Studio, Santa Barbara

Engineered, mixed, and mastered by Emmet Sargeant